A PARENT'S GUIDE to
Lies
Boys
Believe
AND the EPIC QUEST FOR TRUTH

FOREWORD BY ROBERT WOLGEMUTH

A PARENT'S GUIDE to Lies Boys Believe AND THE EPIC QUEST FOR TRUTH

ERIN & JASON DAVIS

NANCY DeMOSS WOLGEMUTH LIES WE BELIEVE SERIES EDITOR

MOODY PUBLISHERS
CHICAGO

Unless otherwise indicated, all Scripture quotations are taken from the *Holy Bible*, New Living Translation, copyright © 1996, 2004, 2015 by Tyndale House Foundation. Used by permission of Tyndale House Publishers, Carol Stream, Illinois 60188. All rights reserved.

Scripture quotations marked (ESV) are from the ESV® Bible (The Holy Bible, English Standard Version®), copyright © 2001 by Crossway, a publishing ministry of Good News Publishers. Used by permission. All rights reserved. The ESV text may not be quoted in any publication made available to the public by a Creative Commons license. The ESV may not be translated in whole or in part into any other language.

All emphasis in Scripture has been added.

Published in association with the literary agency of Wolgemuth & Wilson.

Edited by Amanda Cleary Eastep
Interior and cover design: Erik M. Peterson
Cover camping themed illustrations copyright © 2023 by Artspace /Shutterstock (1090146080). All rights reserved. Cover illustrations of apple copyright © 2023 by Azure_Sun/Shutterstock (1721598025). All rights reserved. Cover illustrations of lined paper copyright © 2023 by Ann Precious/Shutterstock (108187301). All rights reserved. Quiver & arrows illustration copyright © 2023 by ArtMari/Shutterstock (1115229017). All rights reserved. Swiss army knife illustration copyright 2023 by nchjjl/Shutterstock (301645313). All rights reserved. Candy & cup illustration copyright © 2023 by Kysa/ iStock (1456759008). All rights reserved. Shells illustration copyright © 2023 by Silmairel/Shutterstock (281957300). All rights reserved. Sneakers illustration copyright © 2023 by NDanko/Shutterstock (706675984). All rights reserved.
Author photo: Victoria Abel

Printed by: Bethany Press in Bloomington, MN – 08/2023

ISBN: 978-0-8024-2937-7

Originally delivered by fleets of horse-drawn wagons, the affordable paperbacks from D. L. Moody's publishing house resourced the church and served everyday people. Now, after more than 125 years of publishing and ministry, Moody Publishers' mission remains the same—even if our delivery systems have changed a bit. For more information on other books (and resources) created from a biblical perspective, go to www.moodypublishers.com or write to:

Moody Publishers
820 N. LaSalle Boulevard
Chicago, IL 60610

1 3 5 7 9 10 8 6 4 2
Printed in the United States of America

CONTENTS

FOREWORD

In His providence, the Lord did not give me sons. Instead, He chose to send girls. Two of them.

Of course, sons or not, my memory is crisp enough today to remember what it was like to *be* a boy. It was my lot as a lad to face the challenges of being a late-blooming one of six children, growing up as a preacher's kid, spending time with my family on the mission field, unsuccessfully attempting to make it to the next level in school sports, and living with the sense that I was a terminally ordinary boy.

Although my grades were decent, no Ivy League school aggressively sought me.

Insecurities, common to most boys, were all mine. **And, although I have not done any research on this, I'm guessing that most young men see themselves more like sparrows than eagles. This probably describes your boy.**

The job that parents have navigating the twists and turns of birthing and growing an uncertain baby boy into a strong young man are myriad. And no parent—mom or dad—would ever turn away from solid counsel. Especially when it comes from a mother and father who are living on the front lines of this challenge themselves.

You've come to the right place. Such help is here. Jason and Erin Davis, parents of four boys, are poised to come alongside—helping you, guiding you, and encouraging you as they invite your sons into an outdoor adventure story.

As a mom and dad with the smell of boy smoke on their clothing, their wisdom is worth embracing. I promise. But the most important truth you'll learn from this book is that you cannot do this job well alone. The Spirit of the living God can be your companion . . . the source and power you'll need to be the parents He has called you to be.

The starting place for you as you embrace the daunting job of leading the young man in your home well is understanding that this lad isn't just another mouth to feed, another kid to clean up after. He's actually a present, better than any your child will ever find under the Christmas tree.

> Children are a gift from the LORD;
> they are a reward from him. (Psalm 127:3)

Once you know and believe this, the inevitable challenges you are certain to encounter will be opportunities for the Lord to use your availability and, yes, your weaknesses for His glory, through your boy.

Jason and Erin are your friends. Shoulders to cry on and wise advisers to lead you to the wisdom you're seeking. And needing.

You're going to love this guide and the book it companions. And even though it may take a while until he actually thanks you for taking time to soak in its good advice, someday he will.

ROBERT WOLGEMUTH
Dad and bestselling author

> I could have no greater joy than to hear
> that my children are following the truth.
> 3 John 4

CHAPTER 1:
Getting Started

To help you keep pace with your son, each chapter in this Parent's Guide corresponds with the specific section your boys should be reading in the *Lies Boys Believe* book. For instance, this chapter (Chapter 1: Getting Started) will equip you to discuss your child's reading of "Meet Your Guides" in the book.

What Your Son Is Reading in *Lies Boys Believe*:

Meet Your Guides!

Sometimes, a near death experience is the best way to get your son's attention. Let us explain.

Before we do, we should probably introduce ourselves.

We're Jason and Erin Davis, high school sweethearts who boomeranged back to our hometown when it was time to raise a family of our own. In our case, that meant we had to give up the perks of city life—like good restaurants, a wide variety of educational options, drive-thru coffee, and even a Walmart—to live in a tiny town of about 4,000 people, most of whom are fond of telling us, "I've known you since you were knee high to a grasshopper." We live in a fifty-year-old farmhouse built by my (Jason's) grandfather. We eat eggs from our coop, butcher our own beef, and can always tell when the blackberries are ripe because our children start walking around with deep purple stains on their teeth.

Farm livin' may not be the life for you, but we're confident that you want the same things for your son(s) that we want for ours: *deep roots.* Speaking of sons . . . we have four of them. Every time we went to the delivery room we heard a doctor say the same remarkable sentence:

"It's a boy!"
"It's a boy!"
"It's a boy!"
"It's . . . another . . . boy!"

Those boys aren't swaddled in soft blankets or playing peek-a-boo anymore. As we write these words, our oldest son, Eli, is learning to drive. Our second son, Noble, recently blew out thirteen candles on his birthday cake. Judah is nine and our resident comedian; and our youngest son, Ezra, is still a little guy. Always eager to do what his big brothers do, he doesn't seem to know that he's only four.

While we are grateful to watch our children play on the same red metal slide we loved as kids and spend their summers catching crawdads with their cousins, proximity to family and embracing small town life aren't the kind of roots we most want to see developed in our boys. We long for them to have deep *spiritual roots*, the kind that draw strength from the aquifer of living water that Jesus described in John 7:38:

> "Anyone who believes in me may come and drink! For the Scriptures declare, 'Rivers of living water will flow from his heart.'"

We wrote this book because the *deep roots of faith* are the ones boys need most desperately to keep them firmly grounded in the Truth as they grow from boys to men.

Rooted in God's Love

Listen to the words the apostle Paul wrote to his spiritual children at the church in Ephesus:

> When I think of all this, I fall to my knees and pray to the Father, the Creator of everything in heaven and on earth. I pray that from his glorious, unlimited resources he will empower you with inner strength through his Spirit. *Then*

Christ will make his home in your hearts as you trust in him. Your roots will grow down into God's love and keep you strong. And may you have the power to understand, as all God's people should, how wide, how long, how high, and how deep his love is. May you experience the love of Christ, though it is too great to understand fully. Then you will be made complete with all the fullness of life and power that comes from God. (Ephesians 3:14–19)

It was a very parental kind of prayer, wasn't it? Paul's desire to see the baby Christians he was writing to live tethered to God's Truth drove him to his knees. He was saying, essentially, "Choose Jesus! He will keep you from being swept away by the lies of this world. He loves you so much and I do too!"

Our boys are growing up in a deceived world. So many of the things that our parents were able to shield us from, including gender-bending social norms, scary information funneled through social media, and ideals about masculinity and femininity that are completely foreign to God's Word are in the air our sons are breathing. *Sooner rather than later they are going to encounter lies.* They'll need the right tools to choose Truth. Here's hope: *you* can equip your son to stand firm.

Though Scripture has promised that you have everything you need for life and godliness (2 Peter 1:3), *Lies Boys Believe* and this companion Parent's Guide are tools you can add to the resources God has given you as you choose Truth as a family.

We will never claim to have raising boys all figured out. I (Erin) am fond of saying that I'm just a cracked pot, raising cracked pots. We're *all* broken by sin and in desperate need of God's grace. But we're thrilled to be your guides on this journey to teach your son to know and love God's Truth. What an adventure it will be!

Which takes us back to the near death experience . . .

Face the Hard Stuff Head-On

When our oldest son, Eli, turned thirteen, we promised him a father-son road trip. No girls. No siblings. No rules. Just me (Jason) and my son, lots of gas station snacks, and ten days packed with new memories. It's a rite of passage we repeated with our second son, Noble, when he turned thirteen, and plan to repeat again with the other two.

Eli and I packed up our family's big white van and headed west. Eli had never seen the mountains before, and I'd spent years dreaming of the day when I could watch his eyes grow wide with wonder as he took in the Rockies for the first time. The moment was everything I'd hoped it would be, one of many times I've savored the blessing of watching one of my sons experience God's goodness through the remarkable world He has made.

As part of that trip, we decided to take our twelve-passenger, rear-wheel-drive van up a trail that was definitely *not* made for vehicles like ours. I didn't tell Eli at the time (I was too busy trying to avoid plummeting off of the side of the mountain!), but I wasn't sure how we were going to make it. With God's help, we did. We have laughed about that excursion many times since. I wouldn't do it again, even if you offered me a big juicy steak with a side of crispy fries when we made it back down, but I wouldn't trade that memory either. My son and I faced something challenging head-on. Together, we held on to what was true:

- I know how to drive in difficult situations.

- The brakes worked.

- There was no need to rush.

- Jesus was with us. He would help us.

There is a parenting parallel at play here. While we understand the temptation to adopt a head-in-the-sand posture when it comes to the lies our children are facing, that won't protect them from being deceived. We've got to face this head-on, side by side, grounded in the Truth and confident that *God is with us. He will help us.*

Your Family Is a Spiritual Formation Machine

If there is one constant in parenting, it is feeling under-equipped. We will never forget what it felt like to be discharged from the hospital after Eli was born. Still in our twenties, no book or class could prepare us for the reality that we were now in charge of this tiny person twenty-four hours a day. We looked at each other and looked at our six-pound, six-ounce teeny-weeny baby boy and knew that with God's help, we'd figure it out. A similar scenario has played out many times in our parenting journey.

- When we didn't know how to buy groceries with one boy outside the cart, one boy inside the cart in a punkin' seat, and one boy in a baby carrier, God helped and we figured it out.

- When we didn't know how to cope when everyone, including us, got the flu at the same time, God helped and we figured it out.

- When we didn't know how to handle our boys' new preteen mood swings, God helped and we figured it out.

- When one of our sons was exposed to pornography on a friend's phone and we didn't know how to help him understand the seriousness without shaming him, God helped and we figured it out.

And when you don't know what lies your son is believing or how to keep him grounded in the Truth, God will help and you will figure it out. **You are the one God has chosen for the job of discipling your son in this stage of life.**

Let us have the privilege of challenging you to set the parenting bar higher than just raising good kids. (Which is a daunting task on its own!) Your children didn't come into the world knowing God. They weren't born reaching for His Word. In partnership with the Holy Spirit those are things that must be taught, preferably at a young age. That makes our homes ground zero for spiritual formation.

Forming your son into a man who can recognize a lie, resist it, and replace it with Truth won't just happen, but it's a skill he can learn when you live intentionally in the incubator of your family life.

Returning Fire

We're going to talk a lot about God's enemy, Satan, in the next chapter. You will probably think a lot about him and the ways he targets your son with lies as you work through this guide. It may make you feel angry, but it ought not make you feel helpless.

In *Lies Men Believe*, Robert Wolgemuth wrote:

> Don't let fear keep you from the battle, but trust in our Commander. Don't settle for a clean stable and an unfurrowed field if He wants to give you an abundant harvest. Remember that, because of our children, we are changing the world, one child—one diaper—at a time.
>
> **The Truth: Children are a gift from the Lord; He wants to use them to spread the gospel in our messed-up world. When I embrace children as a gift, I partner with God in changing that world.**[1]

Robert was repeating the gist of something King David wrote.

> Children are a gift from the LORD;
>   they are a reward from him.
> Children born to a young man
>   are like arrows in a warrior's hands.
> How joyful is the man whose quiver is full of them!
>   He will not be put to shame when he confronts his
>   accusers at the city gates.
> (Psalm 127:3–5)

Through His Word, God calls you to fight for the hearts of your children and to fight alongside your children in the battle for Truth.

---

1. Robert Wolgemuth, *Lies Men Believe: And the Truth That Sets Them Free* (Chicago: Moody Publishers, 2018), 178.

May you often be struck by the realities of missionary Jim Elliot's famous words:

> Remember how the Psalmist described children? He said that they were as an heritage from the Lord, and that every man should be happy who had his quiver full of them. And what is a quiver full of but arrows? And what are arrows for but to shoot? **So, with the strong arms of prayer, draw the bowstring back and let the arrows fly—all of them, straight at the Enemy's hosts.**[2]

How to Use This Book

We chose to write *Lies Boys Believe* as a work of fiction because our sons love graphic novels. Your son's book follows a dad and his two sons, Lenny and Thomas, on an exciting cross-country adventure a lot like the one Eli and I took as his rite of passage into the teenage years. Though we pulled from many of the characteristics of ourselves and our kids, *the book is a work of fiction.*

Each chapter also features a **Tag, You're It!** section. These are opportunities for your son to digest what he's learning through Bible reading and engaging activities. While we hope your boy is gripped by the story element and can't wait to discover

---

2. As quoted by J. D. Greear, "A Letter from Jim Elliot to His Parents," January 8, 2014, https://jdgreear.com/a-letter-from-jim-elliot-to-his-parents/. Emphasis added.

what happens next, encourage him not to skip the interactive segments. There's gold in them thar hills!

You have already taken an important step toward helping your son live free from lies by getting a copy of *Lies Boys Believe* for him and digging into this companion guide for yourself. We know that resources are precious, and we're confident that the investment of time and money you're making will matter. Here's how to get the most out of it.

Read *A Parent's Guide to Lies Boys Believe* at the same time or pace that your son reads *Lies Boys Believe*. Because the format of *Lies Boys Believe* is fiction and interactive, we'd suggest that you make it a part of your family reading routine. Other siblings will get a lot out of it too, even if they're much older or younger than the boy you had in mind for this journey. (If you have girls, we highly recommend *Lies Girls Believe* written by our dear friend Dannah Gresh).

Parameters for what your son should be reading are indicated as **What Your Son Is Reading** at the beginning of each chapter of this guide.

Pray for your son daily. As parents, prayer is our primary work. Of course, we need to teach our sons how to brush their teeth, help them with their math homework, aim their hearts in the right direction, and discipline them. All of that is a necessary part of life with kids. But while prayer can often feel like a nonessential in a day with many demands, it's the most important thing you can do for your son. *Prayer changes things!* Scripture reveals that God is attentive to the prayers offered up by parents on their children's behalf. Since prayer is one parent (you) talking to another parent (your heavenly Father), prayer prompts throughout this book will look like this.

PARENT TO PARENT

In Isaiah 61:3 God describes the children of Israel this way:

> In their righteousness, they will be like great oaks
> that the LORD has planted for his own glory.

Pray for your son to:

- Pursue righteous (holy) living

- Grow into a mighty man of God, strong and secure

- Have deep roots that keep him from being tossed by the lies of the world

- Glorify God with his life

Commit to pray for your son every day as you journey through this resource. We will provide prayer ideas in each chapter. In response to what you're learning, what your child is sharing, and what the Holy Spirit is stirring in your heart, simply talk to God about what you want to see Him do in your son's life.

Talk about lies and Truth—often!

As we've written these books, we've prayed that they would lead to meaningful and transformative conversations between a boy and his parents. And yet, we know from experience that parents don't get to choose if and when their child opens up. As a mom, I (Erin) have noticed the signal when my love for conversation has overwhelmed my sons. A telltale look of confusion mixed with boredom comes over their eyes. Kids don't want to be rude, but they have reached the limit of how many words they can absorb. (As the only woman in a house full of men, you can imagine how verbose I can be!) I've also learned that the moment they hop in the van with me after school is not the best time to drill them with questions about their day. Every child is different. Some of ours will talk your ear clean off. Some are so quiet we have to make sure they're in the car when we leave home. Some are early birds. Others can't seem to form a coherent sentence before noon. The point is: don't force it.

We'll offer some open-ended questions for each chapter to help start conversations with your son. They'll look like this.

TALK ABOUT IT TOGETHER

Living out God's Truth is a lifelong pursuit. Don't feel like you must talk about everything right now. Remember: your first and most important role in your son's journey toward freedom is to pray. Aren't you glad you can trust the Holy Spirit to do the heavy lifting of transformation? We are too!

Take the time to write out a prayer asking God to work in your son's heart (and in your own) throughout this journey. Consider giving him that prayer along with a short note about why you're proud of him for choosing to take on the challenge of understanding lies and replacing them with God's Truth.

Dear Son,

CHAPTER 2:
This Is Bigger Than Your Boy

> **What Your Son Is Reading** in *Lies Boys Believe*:
>
> ## The Adventure Begins!

It's a running joke at our house that all parents want to know the answer to two questions:

1. Is this normal?

2. How long will it last?

When it comes to falling for lies, the unfortunate answer to question number 1 is yes. Though all people are made in the image of God and deeply loved by God, because of the impact of sin on our lives, all of us are also prone to abandoning truth for lies.

Before we tackle why (or rather *who*), let's start with a working definition of Truth. **Your son will cover this same ground in chapter one of his book.**

LIE (verb)	TRUTH (noun)
To make an untrue statement with intent to deceive.	The real facts about something: the things that are true.

Pretty straightforward, right? Truth is true and a lie . . . isn't? But it's not always easy to tell the difference. How can you know if something is true? Read what Jesus said in John 17:17:

"Your word is truth." (ESV)

When a builder begins a new project, he establishes a plumb line that becomes the standard by which all other measurements are tested. Consider the prophet's words in Isaiah 28:17:

I will test you with the measuring line of justice
  and the plumb line of righteousness.
Since your refuge is made of lies,
  a hailstorm will knock it down.
Since it is made of deception,
  a flood will sweep it away. (emphasis added)

The Bible is your plumb line for Truth. It is the standard by which all other ideas, thoughts, beliefs, and statements must be measured. By helping your son grow his appetite and understanding, you are equipping him to notice when something is "off plumb" in his life.

We live in a culture that normalizes lying and is skeptical of those who frame Truth in black and white. Our modern vernacular ascribes pronouns to truth as if it's relative. While the ideas of "my truth" and "your truth" are embraced, the concept of absolute Truth is often strongly resisted.

Though we certainly face new challenges, we are not the first generation to wonder why our children are so easily deceived. We can trace that back to the very first parents: Adam and Eve.

Read Genesis 2:16–17 and Genesis 3:1 in your Bible. Your son has this same reading assignment in his book.

We can learn a lot about lies from these three verses:

Satan is a liar. Here in Genesis, the Bible describes Satan as shrewd or crafty. It's an image of a sleazy salesman, willing to manipulate the Truth to close the deal. In the New Testament, Jesus described His ancient enemy this way: "He has always hated the truth, because there is no truth in him. When he lies, it is consistent with his character; for he is a liar and the father of lies" (John 8:44).

Satan has his sights set on your boy. We don't know how old the world was when the serpent slithered in, hellbent on deception, but we know who was in his sights. He targeted the first family, the crowns of creation who bore the image of God (Genesis 1:27). **He has relentlessly attacked families ever since.**

Scripture warns us to be watchful for his attacks.

> "Stay alert! Watch out for your great enemy, the devil. He prowls around like a roaring lion, looking for someone to devour." (1 Peter 5:8)

We want to say something here, and we don't necessarily have a specific Bible verse to prove it. Call it a gut feeling produced from several decades of living for Jesus plus a dose of common sense. *Satan seems to target the weak.* Those who are easiest to manipulate. In other words: Satan is gunning for your young son.

Haven't you already seen evidence of this in his life? His young mind lacks the maturity to easily spot lies. He is prone to go along with his peers and sometimes lacks discernment about what is true and what isn't. His body still has some growing to do. In the same way, he may need to grow into the wisdom given in God's Word.

If Satan can derail your son, if only temporarily, during his preteen and teen years, he wins a great victory. Certainly, God is able to redeem our poor choices and draw us back to the

Truth, but how much better it is for your son to never taste the bitter fruit of deception at all!

As Christian parents, it has helped us to stop being surprised by the many ways Satan assaults our sons with lies. Instead of being reactive, in a defensive posture, we've become proactive and on the offensive.

Lies are often difficult to spot. Did you notice how Satan's words to Eve sounded eerily similar to God's?

God said: "You may freely eat the fruit of every tree in the garden—except the tree of the knowledge of good and evil. If you eat its fruit, you are sure to die" (Genesis 2:16–17).

Satan said: "Did God really say you must not eat the fruit from any of the trees in the garden?" (Genesis 3:1).

God said they could eat from *all but one* tree. Satan said they couldn't eat from *any trees*. It was so subtle—easily dismissed as a slip of the tongue. *But this was no accident.* The liar twisted what was of God and made it appear not good.

He may be shrewd, but he isn't very creative. He still lies to God's children. He still targets the ones whose faith is fresh and new. And He still takes what's true and shapes it into something that isn't. Like any good soldier would, you must study the enemy's tactics to effectively fight in the war for your son's heart and mind.

How Lies Become Lifestyles

Here's one more note before you and your son jump into the story—*thoughts based on lies often become actions.*

Jesus' brother wrote about this in James 1:14–16:

> Temptation comes from our own desires, which entice us and drag us away. These desires give birth to sinful actions. And when sin is allowed to grow, it gives birth to death.
>
> So don't be misled, my dear brothers and sisters.

To simplify, let's put that progression in a list.

You have a desire.

You are tempted to fulfill that desire.

The temptation takes the form of an enticing lie.

Which leads to sin.

Which leads to death.

The odometer of your life probably has enough miles on it to affirm this progression. You can reflect on times when you were in bondage to sin and trace them back to a willingness to believe a lie in order to fulfill a desire.

Not all desires are bad. Your son has a desire to:

- Be loved

- Be accepted

- Be respected by other young men

- Prove that he has what it takes

- Be brave

- Lead others

When those desires intersect with a lie crafted by Satan for your son's destruction, your boy is on a trajectory toward bondage. In learning how to identify lies and replace them with God's Truth, he is learning how to turn his feet away from sin and run hard toward godliness.

The stakes are sky high, but so are the rewards. If your son can learn to resist the enemy's lies and love God's Word at an early age, the victory is huge!

PARENT TO PARENT

James 4:7–8 says, "So humble yourselves before God. Resist the devil, and he will flee from you. Come close to God, and God will come close to you."

Pray for your son to:

- Be humble and know that he needs help to recognize and turn from lies

- Resist the devil

- Come close to God

- Experience the presence of God in his life.

TALK ABOUT IT TOGETHER

Prayerfully watch for opportunities to chat with your son about the Truth you've both learned in the chapters you've read. Here are some open-ended questions to get you started. Some are silly to break the ice. Others go for the spiritual jugular. We find our sons are more willing to open up when we're having fun, so we recommend a mix of light and heavy questions.

- How do you like your marshmallow cooked?

- Describe the perfect s'more.

- Let's play two truths and a lie. I'll go first!

- What did you learn about Satan in your chapter? Did anything that you learned surprise you?

- How can you tell if something is true?

- What do you think it means that God's Word is Truth? How does that impact your daily life?

One More Thing

This book is part of a family of books dedicated to helping God's people turn from the bondage of lies and live in freedom, including:

Lies Women Believe by Nancy DeMoss Wolgemuth

Lies Young Women Believe by Nancy DeMoss Wolgemuth and Dannah Gresh

Lies Girls Believe by Dannah Gresh

Lies Men Believe by Robert Wolgemuth

If you haven't read these books, please consider picking up a copy and growing in your own understanding of what it means to walk in Truth. **There is no greater tool you can give your son to help him walk in freedom than to have a life-transforming encounter with Truth yourself.**

Find all of the books in this series at LiesBooks.com.

CHAPTER 3:
Developing Delight for God's Word

What Your Son Is Reading in *Lies Boys Believe*:

LIE #1: "Reading the Bible just isn't for me."

TRUTH: The Bible is your treasure!

When we remodeled our farmhouse, we stripped it down to the bare bones. Flooring was ripped up, wallpaper was torn off, and *everything* got a fresh coat of paint. A small army of friends and family worked tirelessly for weeks helping us transform dated spaces into the home in which we've since made so many memories.

At one point in the project, I (Erin) asked the whole crew to stop working. Silence fell suddenly as saws stopped buzzing and hammers stopped swinging. I handed out Sharpies and asked everyone to cover the surfaces of our home in Scripture and words of blessing for our family.

You wouldn't know it now, but written on every subfloor and hidden under the paint on most of our walls are some of our favorite passages of God's Word. Eli was just a toddler and Noble was still in diapers at the time. Judah and Ezra joined our family years later. Even though they weren't there and their brothers were too young to remember it, the decision to write God's Word on our home has had a lasting impact on their lives. It is a real-life metaphor for our desire to build our family on the solid foundation of God's Word.

Raising sons who love the Bible can feel like a daunting assignment, especially when you're not having any luck teaching them how to wipe the toothpaste gloop from the sink. Still, it's not as complex as we tend to make it.

Consider the parenting model found in Deuteronomy 6:4–9:

> "Listen, O Israel! The LORD is our God, the LORD alone. And you must love the LORD your God with all your heart, all your soul, and all your strength. And you must commit yourselves wholeheartedly to these commands that I am giving you today. Repeat them again and again to your

children. Talk about them when you are at home and when you are on the road, when you are going to bed and when you are getting up. Tie them to your hands and wear them on your forehead as reminders. Write them on the doorposts of your house and on your gates."

Don't rush past this. Pause and marvel at the fact that these words were penned nearly three thousand years ago in an ancient Middle Eastern culture; and yet, they still provide practical wisdom for parenting today. Let's break it down.

1. God is God. There is no other (v. 4).

2. He has called you—*yes, you*—to love Him with everything you've got (v. 5). This is your first and most important job as a parent.

3. Commit yourself fully to God's commands, which are found in His Word. Don't do it halfway.

4. Repeat God's Word again and again (and again!) to your children.

5. Here's how: Talk about Scripture as you go about your everyday life. Talk about the Word at home, in the car, at bedtime, and at the breakfast table. Surround your homestead with God's letters from your true home, heaven.

Notice how God did not command us to have family devotions where everyone can find the book of Habakkuk easily and all children are well-behaved. (What a relief!) He didn't give us a one-size-fits-all formula. Instead, God calls us to a *lifestyle* and a *lifetime* of knowing and teaching His Word.

As our children progress through the various stages of childhood and as our lives ebb and flow in intensity and busyness, we've had to adjust how we do this many times. More important than *how* you grow your son's love for Scripture is *that* you grow your son's love for Scripture. He's learning that the Bible is his treasure. **Is it yours?**

Psalm 119 is the longest psalm in the Bible. Although no author is named, one tradition holds that King David penned this psalm as a way to teach his young son Solomon the alphabet, since the twenty-two stanzas each begin with a different Hebrew letter. Like instructions found in Deuteronomy 6, David seized the opportunity to teach his son God's Truth while he was doing a routine parenting task. In verse 24, he taught his son to say,

> "Your testimonies are my delight; they are my counselors." (ESV)

Go back and circle that word "delight." That's your North Star for helping your son treasure God's Word. *Reading the Bible is not a duty; there are no meaningless chores in the Christian life.* For him to treasure God's Word, he must delight in God's Word. You can help him by looking for ways to make engaging with Scripture exciting, practical, and rewarding.

The Silver Lining of the Biblical Illiteracy Cloud

It's no secret that biblical literacy among adults in Western countries is on a steep decline, so much so that many are calling it a crisis.[3] We agree that Christians not reading their Bibles is the spiritual equivalent to a five-alarm fire; yet, when we think of our sons and their friends and your sons and their friends, we are filled with hope.

One Barna study that focused on teens and their Bibles found:

- 59 percent have a Bible in their home

- 20 percent read the Bible at least weekly

- 23 percent of those who've made a personal commitment to follow Jesus read their Bible daily

- 22 percent say they don't understand Scripture[4]

Your son may still be a preteen, but, as he will learn in *Lies Boys Believe*, he is who he is becoming. Bible-reading attitudes and

---

3. Jeffery Fulks, Randy Petersen, and John Farquhar Plake, "State of the Bible USA 2022," American Bible Society, January 2023, https://1s712.americanbible.org/state-of-the-bible/stateofthebible/State_of_the_bible-2022.pdf.

4. Diana Chandler, "Teens Hold High View of Bible but Don't Read It Often, Barna Finds," Baptist Press, October 12, 2022, https://www.baptistpress.com/resource-library/news/teens-hold-high-view-of-bible-but-dont-read-it-often-barna-finds.

habits formed now will bear fruit (for better or worse) in his teen years and beyond. No doubt, the 23 percent of teenagers who read their Bibles regularly likely learned to delight in God's Word years before.

As you help your son cultivate a delight for Scripture, consider your own approach to the Bible. Is reading it a daily habit or are you inconsistent? Do your children see you reading the Bible? Are there ways—such as reading a daily proverb at the breakfast table or making Scripture reading a part of your child's bedtime routine—that you can "talk about [the Bible] when you are at home and when you are on the road, when you are going to bed and when you are getting up"?

PARENT TO PARENT

Through the acrostic we now know as Psalm 119, any parent can teach their son that the path to pure thoughts and actions is loving and living God's Word. Pray through the adaptation of Psalm 119:9–16 below, inserting your son's name where fitting.

How can [your son] keep his way pure?
By guarding it according to Your Word.

Help him seek You with his whole heart;
  let him not wander from Your commandments!

Help him store up Your Word in his heart,
  that he might not sin against You.

Blessed are You, O Lord;
  teach [your son's name] Your statutes!

With his lips help him declare
  all the rules of Your mouth.

Help me teach him to delight in Your testimonies
  as much as in all riches.

I will meditate on Your precepts
  and fix my eyes on Your ways.

Help me teach my son to do the same.

We delight in Your statutes;
  we will not forget Your Word.

TALK ABOUT IT TOGETHER

Prayerfully watch for opportunities to chat with your son about the Truth you've learned in the chapters you've both read.

• Have you ever packed up a tent? Tell me about it.

• What's your greatest treasure?

- How would you feel if you went into the mine and discovered the "treasure" was a Bible?

- Does the Bible ever seem boring or hard to understand to you?

- What do you think "Feelings aren't facts" means? How does it apply to reading the Bible?

- Did you take the 30-day challenge? Why or why not? How can I help you keep your commitment?

CHAPTER 4:
The Greatest Gift
You Can Give Your Son

A younger couple we adore recently came to our house for a visit to share the news that they were pregnant with their first child. They asked a lot of new parenting questions like:

- What should we put on our baby shower registry?
- How did you decide what you named your sons?

• Can we raise a baby in our apartment? Should we be looking for a house?

We smiled compassionately as our own memories of becoming parents floated to the surface of our hearts. We assured them that as it applies to parenting, it all comes out in the wash, and they'd figure it out one step at a time.

The new dad's eyes filled with sudden tears. "What's it like to tell your kids about Jesus?" he asked.

"Remarkable," we assured him.

"I can't wait," he said with an eager smile.

Isn't that the goal of running the gauntlet required to get them to church every week (preferably with shoes on), signing them up for Vacation Bible School, and reading from their storybook Bible each night? As Christian parents, we affirm the words of 3 John 4: "I could have no greater joy than to hear that my children are following the truth."

Though witnessing our children accept Jesus as their Savior is a moment we've long prayed for, we couldn't help but fear we'd mess it up. You might be facing that same angst as you prepare to talk with your son about the gospel as he digests what he's reading. Let us give you a little pep talk: you probably will "mess it up." How's that for peppy? The good news is that sharing the gospel isn't about saying specific words in a specific order. It's not about praying a certain prayer, and—here's the best news— it's the Holy Spirit's job to open your son's eyes to his need for Jesus. You are off the hook for creating true heart change.

The term "gospel" can be thrown around like a hot potato among Christians. Even though your own life has been transformed by it, it can be difficult to articulate what the gospel is. Part of that is because it is a supernatural work of God, but part of that is because we tend to make it too complicated. Let's review the basics.

The gospel is:

1. All people are sinners (Romans 3:23) prone to run in rebellion (Isaiah 53:6) away from the boundaries God has lovingly set (Psalm 19:7–9).

2. Because God is holy, our sin separates us from Him (Isaiah 59:1–2).

3. The righteous punishment for sin is death (Romans 6:23). We need to be rescued or "saved" from the punishment that we deserve.

4. Jesus went to the cross to take on our punishment. Because of His death, we have been spared the death penalty (2 Corinthians 5:21).

5. In response to our great need and Christ's great sacrifice, we surrender our lives to God's authority (Galatians 2:20), repent of our sin (Acts 3:19), and seek to live God-honoring lives (Matthew 6:33).

Or, in the beautiful words of John Newton, "I am a great sinner and Christ is a great Savior." (Newton went on to write the famous hymn *Amazing Grace*.)

Leading Wild Hearts to Jesus

Eli was nine when he started peppering me (Erin) with questions about his sin and Jesus' forgiveness from the back seat of the van. By the time I put the van in park, I could tell that he understood his need for a Savior and was ready to crown Jesus the King of his life. His daddy baptized him on Easter morning. It was one of the highlights of our lives.

Noble made the same decision a couple of years later. Jason baptized him in a river while family and friends watched from a gravel bar. It was another defining moment for our family.

Our second born has always lived up to his name. He truly is a noble Noble—noble and very tender. The rest of us are rowdy and not exactly prone to coloring within the lines of life. By contrast, Noble seems to live by the motto "Don't rock the boat." We used to call him Noble the repenter. He would come to us with the sob sobs.

"What's wrong?" we'd ask.

"I" sob sob "thought about" sob sob "hitting my" sob sob "brother" sob sob sob sob.

Honestly, it was hard not to laugh. Since the brothers on either side of him in the family pecking order are much more . . . shall we say . . . spirited, we'd assure him that until he actually sinned, he didn't need to come and tell us. Even as he heads into his teen years, he still has that sensitive conscience. We pray he never loses it.

The flipside of that kind of wiring is that it's easy to think of yourself as "good" compared to other people. He gets good grades, never gets in trouble at school and rarely at home. He is the poster child for being a "good boy." For Noble, the most challenging part of the gospel is recognizing that he needs a Savior too. By God's standard, even good boys aren't good enough to be right with God. As his parents, we've helped him wrestle with what the Bible says when it states, "No one is righteous—not even one" (Romans 3:10).

We were enjoying shrimp dinner on the shore when Judah professed his faith in Christ. Why then? Who knows! He just decided he was ready. We talked through the gospel with him again. It was clear he *was* ready to accept that he needed a Savior. We paid our check, walked out into the ocean, and Jason baptized Judah in sparkling waters as a choir of seagulls sang overhead.

As we write this book, Ezra is still very small. He loves going to church, hears nightly stories from his storybook Bible, and knows that Jesus loves him.

Daily rhythms that point your son to the gospel are seeds of eternal significance. As you continue to plant and tend to the Truth of both your son's need and Christ's great love, seedlings of faith will begin to grow.

As you and your son live the gospel this week, offer God fresh prayers of gratitude that He invites you to be a part of the redeeming work He is doing in your child's life.

PARENT TO PARENT

Often called the "Romans Road," a collection of verses in the New Testament book of Romans outlines the gospel . . . the plan of salvation. Consider talking through these verses with your son and/or praying through them for your son.

Romans 3:23: Everyone has sinned; we all fall short of God's glorious standard.

Romans 6:23: For the wages of sin is death, but the free gift of God is eternal life through Christ Jesus our Lord.

Romans 10:9: If you openly declare that Jesus is Lord and believe in your heart that God raised him from the dead, you will be saved.

Romans 5:1: Therefore, since we have been made right in God's sight by faith, we have peace with God because of what Jesus Christ our Lord has done for us.

TALK ABOUT IT TOGETHER

Prayerfully watch for opportunities to chat with your son about the Truth you've learned in the chapters you've both read.

- Do you think it would be fun to be a cowboy for a day? What would be your favorite part?

- Do you ever want to disobey the rules? Why do you think that is?

- What's the difference between being "good" and being right with God?

- Can you tell me what the gospel means?

- Have you ever said you're sorry for your sins and asked Jesus to be in charge of your life? Why or why not?

- Is there anything you're worried God won't forgive you for?

CHAPTER 5:
Building a "No Secrets" Family

What Your Son Is Reading in *Lies Boys Believe*:

LIE #3: "No one needs to know about my sin."

TRUTH: Telling your story to someone and admitting your sin sets you free.

(Erin) *almost* got away with it.

It was the last day of school of my sophomore year in high school. My newfound freedom as a licensed driver emboldened me, and I challenged my friend Angie to a race. I won, but only because she got pulled over going 75 miles per hour in a

60 mile per hour zone. Knowing how much trouble I'd be in if my parents discovered I'd been driving recklessly, I made up a cover story to avoid getting in trouble. It worked . . . temporarily.

Unfortunately for me, my sister was in Angie's car. As part of her punishment, Angie had to face the parents of every girl she'd put in danger by driving so fast. She and her mom came to our house, and Angie said something like, "I am sorry I put your daughters in danger by racing. I won't do it again."

My mom smiled at Angie. Then she smiled at me in the kind of way that let me know we'd be talking about this when Angie and her family left. Suffice it to say, I didn't get to do much driving for a long time after that.

If you take a moment to consider your own childhood, you can likely remember the feeling of doing something you weren't supposed to and fearing you'd be found out. Whether it was taking something that didn't belong to you, breaking something that your parents treasured, or being somewhere you weren't supposed to be . . . there is a certain sweaty-palms, dry-mouth, racing-heart reaction we have when we're trying to keep a secret.

Covering tracks is an impulse most children have. We can trace that reflex all the way back to ground zero for lies. **Open your Bible and read Genesis 3:6–12.**

The first lie ⟶ followed by the first sin ⟶ followed by the first cover-up. It's laughable really. In sinning, Adam and Eve had essentially dropped a nuclear bomb on God's creation, the fallout of which is still wreaking havoc today. But they thought they could cover it up with fig leaves and playing hide-and-seek.

Like creating an environment for dangerous bacteria to grow, secrets produce shame, which leads to more secrets, which leads to isolation, which leads to deception, which leads to bondage.

In order to become a family who resists the enemy's lies and lives for Truth, you must proactively adopt a "no secrets" policy.

When There's Frosting Under the Bed

Several months ago, I (Erin) decided to deep clean our sons' rooms while they were at school. When I say "deep clean," I mean deeeeeep clean, and this time that involved pulling out everything that was stashed under their beds.

In addition to several single socks (where does the other one go?), piles of LEGO® bricks, a few army men who had gone AWOL, and the library books we thought we'd looked everywhere for, I found a box of secrets.

It contained:

1. A half eaten jar of chocolate frosting

2. Several empty bags of chocolate chips

3. A few dried marshmallows

4. Enough candy wrappers to fill a drinking cup

5. And a few plastic string cheese wrappers

Clearly, the son whose bed the box was under had been sneaking snacks, especially the sugary kind.

When he got home from school, I showed him the box and gave him a punishment.

"What's the big deal?" he protested. "It's just snacks!"

I explained that it wasn't about the food. Though we strive for moderation, our kids are allowed to eat sugar. If he was hungry at bedtime, we would have been happy to accommodate. *The problem was the sneaking.*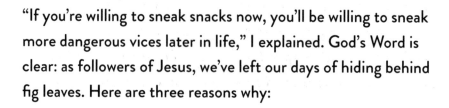

"If you're willing to sneak snacks now, you'll be willing to sneak more dangerous vices later in life," I explained. God's Word is clear: as followers of Jesus, we've left our days of hiding behind fig leaves. Here are three reasons why:

1. There are *no secrets* with God.

God knew Adam and Eve were hiding in the bushes. He made everything. He *sees* everything. There wasn't a leaf or twig large enough to hide them from Him.

Jesus was teaching about prayer when He said, "Your Father, *who sees everything*, will reward you (Matthew 6:6).

The psalmist wrote,

> My frame was not hidden from you,
> when I was being made in secret,
>   intricately woven in the depths of the earth.
> (Psalm 139:15 ESV)

Proverbs 15:11 declares,

> Even Death and Destruction hold no secrets from the LORD.
> How much more does he know the human heart!

God sees. God knows. While that should inject a healthy dose of fear into our hearts, it should also liberate us from any illusion that we can cover up our sin. We can model this with our children by openly confessing our sin to them (more on that in a moment), responding in Christlike ways when they confess their sin to us, and openly opposing secret-keeping.

2. God's people are called to live in the light.

> This is the message we heard from Jesus and now declare to you: God is light, and there is no darkness in him at all. So we are lying if we say we have fellowship with God but go on living in spiritual darkness; we are not practicing the truth. But if we are living in the light, as God is in the light, then we have fellowship with each other, and the blood of Jesus, his Son, cleanses us from all sin. (1 John 1:5–7)

Throughout Scripture, light is used as a descriptor for sin-free-ness (a.k.a. holiness). Just as sunshine is the best disinfectant, living our lives in openness, free from secrets, reveals sin and helps us to turn from it.

God goes beyond simply dwelling in the light—*He is light*. Psalm 104:2 says that He is wrapped in a robe of light. First Timothy 6:16 tells us, "He lives in light so brilliant that no human can approach him." Ephesians 5:13 warns us that all sin will ultimately be exposed by Christ's light.

By refusing to hide sins, desires, habits, or heartbreaks, you are modeling to your children who God is.

3. Scripture invites you into a rhythm of confession and forgiveness.

Nothing exposes your sin nature quite like becoming a parent. It's natural to think things like: "I was never angry until I had kids," or "I didn't struggle with irritability until I became a mom," or "I wouldn't be so out of control if I could just get some sleep!" But the reality is that you are a born sinner. Parenting is simply the circumstance God is using to expose the depravity that exists in your heart. That can be discouraging, but God has provided an escape from becoming a parent constantly riddled with guilt: "Confess your sins to each other and pray for each other so that you may be healed. The earnest prayer of a righteous person has great power and produces wonderful results" (James 5:16).

This is not a once-and-done mandate. It's a lifestyle. As the parent, you can lead the charge by regularly owning your mistakes, confessing them as sin, and, if they were involved in the infraction, asking for forgiveness, then praying with your children.

You can also create an environment of grace. That doesn't mean your children will never face consequences. Discipline is not divorced from grace (Hebrews 12:6), but you can seize moments of confession as opportunities to remind your child that they can never lose God's love and they can never lose your love, and to teach them that confession leads to freedom.

PARENT TO PARENT

Ephesians 5:8 says, "For once you were full of darkness, but now you have light from the Lord. So live as people of light!"

Pray for:

- The Spirit to help your son resist darkness and live as a person of the light.

- God to expose any sin in your child's life quickly, helping him turn from it before it becomes a pattern.

- Your family to build patterns of confession and repentance.

TALK ABOUT IT TOGETHER

Prayerfully watch for opportunities to chat with your son about the Truth you've both learned in the chapters you've read.

- If we had a slingshot competition, who do you think would win?

- What is sin? Why is it a big deal?

- How do you know when there's something you need to tell Mom and Dad about?

- Is there anything I can do to make telling me about your sin easier? [We have friends who told their children that if they tell the truth "the first time," there would be no punishment. Consequences or replacement if they broke something, but no punishment. Sometimes this freed them to own up immediately.]

- Why do you think the Bible tells us to confess our sins to one another? Isn't telling Jesus enough?

CHAPTER 6:
God Doesn't Own a Wetsuit

> **What Your Son Is Reading in *Lies Boys Believe*:**
>
> ## LIE #4: "God is always mad at me."
> ## TRUTH: God forgives!

As Nancy DeMoss Wolgemuth and Dannah Gresh were preparing to write *Lies Young Women Believe*, I (Erin) had the privilege of conducting nationwide focus groups. In big cities and small towns, in groups made up of girls with varied backgrounds, family sizes, and educational backgrounds, girls told me over and over about how they struggled to trust God because of their experience with their dads. "God is just like my father" became the number-four lie tackled in that book. Nancy and Dannah wrote,

If you have been wounded by a father—or another man you trusted—you may find it difficult to trust God. You may even be afraid of Him or angry with Him. The thought of responding to Him as a Father may be repulsive to you. And yet, Jesus freely called God His Father and instructed His disciples to address Him as their Father. Paul invites believers to call God "Abba," which means "Daddy" (Romans 8:15).

God is a father, but He is not like any man you have ever known.[5]

As you are reading these words, this may or may not ring true for your boy. I hope your son has experienced fatherhood as God intended: as a source of love, security, and stability. If that's the case, pause now to thank God for that blessing. With 50 percent of marriages ending in divorce,[6] your son may be in the fortunate half with a mom and dad to tuck him in together each night.

But perhaps as you read these words, the thought of your boy's view of God being shaped by his view of you or your spouse makes you flinch.

---

5. Nancy DeMoss Wolgemuth and Dannah Gresh, *Lies Young Women Believe: And the Truth That Sets Them Free* (Chicago: Moody Publishers, 2018), 65.

6. "48 Divorce Statistics in the US Including Divorce Rate, Race, & Marriage Length," updated April 12, 2023, https://divorce.com/blog/divorce-statistics/.

Maybe:

- You're a single mom or dad trying to be both to your son, helpless to fix the disastrous wake your parenting partner's choices have left.

- You're the one who's blown it. You've yelled too much and loved too little. You can see now that your shortcomings as a parent have shaped your son's view of God.

- You came to Christ after you had children. You're still learning who God is. You don't know how to train up your son to run to Christ when you're still taking baby steps.

- Your own view of God has been warped by generational sin patterns. You know that you don't want your son to have the same hang-ups, but if you're honest, you're not exactly walking in freedom.

Aren't you glad you and your son have already spent time soaking in the Truth of the gospel?! Jesus said, "Healthy people don't need a doctor—sick people do. I have come to call not those who think they are righteous, but those who know they are sinners" (Mark 2:17).

It is because our view of God is distorted that our need for Truth is so great! **Family life provides constant opportunities to remind each other who God is and turn together toward Truth.**

When our family relationships expose our constant need for a Savior, I (Erin) am reminded that sometimes gospel seeds look like seashells. One of our sons was in preschool when he came home extra hyper. Something in his behavior clued me in to the fact that something was off. I look back at that moment with wonder as one of the times the Holy Spirit most clearly helped me parent. I waited for a quiet moment when I could give my son my undivided attention and asked, "Buddy, is there anything you need to tell Mommy?" Hot tears instantly filled his bright blue eyes. He reached into the pocket of his corduroy pants and pulled out three little white shells he had stolen from the sand and water table.

"I wanted to give them to GG," he confessed.

GG is his grandma and she *loves* the ocean. It was a thoughtful gesture, but one that required him to steal the shells from the playground at school.

Even at his young age, God had gifted him with a conscience. He knew he had taken what wasn't his, and he tried, unsuccessfully, to cover it up. We explained why stealing was wrong, put him in the car, and drove him back to preschool, where he tearfully confessed to his teacher.

Many years later, I still look back at "the shell saga" and smile. In hindsight, I can see more clearly that the real heart work of that parenting moment wasn't teaching our son not to steal (which is important), but rather teaching him about confession and forgiveness.

That particular child was (and sometimes still is) prone to being easily squashed. When forced to face his sin, he can become an Eeyore. "Poor me . . . I will never be good enough . . . nobody loves me." I recognize it in him because it wells up so easily in me.

In that moment of discipline, and many others like it, we started a little dialogue taken from Micah 7:19, which declares that God will throw our sins to the depth of the sea:

Mom or Dad: When you confess your sin, what does God do with it?

Boy: (With coaching) He hurls it into the ocean.

Mom or Dad: And does God own a wetsuit? Is He going to dive down and drag your sin back up?

Boy: No, God doesn't own a wetsuit.

Of course, God can retrieve anything from anywhere any time He wants to. Yet, when Scripture paints a picture of how our heavenly Father responds to our sin, it's an image of (among other things) Him tossing it into the ocean depths with no desire to dredge it back up.

Your son may not be inclined to worry that God is always mad at him. He may face a different distortion, such as:

- God doesn't love me

- God is distant

- God only tolerates me

- God should fix my problems

- God is not enough

No matter what form lies about God take, the solution is the same. Here's one more thought from *Lies Young Women Believe*:

> **All these lies about God are best remedied by the same thing: Study the Bible to get to know Jesus,** who is the "radiance of the glory of God and the exact imprint of his nature" (Hebrews 1:3). When you see Christ as He is, it will be harder to believe things about God that aren't true.[7]

You've already taken steps to help your son understand the true character of God by taking this journey toward Truth. As you continue to open the Bible together day after day, year after year, you are giving your son the gift of knowing God as He truly is, not how our experiences define Him. What a beautiful and lasting gift! (Better than tiny sea shells.)

---

7. Nancy DeMoss Wolgemuth and Dannah Gresh, *Lies Young Women Believe: And the Truth That Sets Them Free* (Chicago: Moody Publishers, 2018), 51.

PARENT TO PARENT

In Psalm 113:5, the psalmist asked a provocative question: "Who can be compared with the LORD our God, who is enthroned on high?"

Who is like God? Who can we compare Him to? Not ourselves. We are made in His image, not the other way around. Admittedly, it can be hard to picture a God we've never seen. Yet, the psalmist went on to record what he *did* know about God and drew a firm conclusion:

> He stoops to look down
>> on heaven and on earth.
> He lifts the poor from the dust
>> and the needy from the garbage dump.
> He sets them among princes,
>> even the princes of his own people!
> He gives the childless woman a family,
>> making her a happy mother.

Praise the LORD! (Psalm 113:6–9)

Pray for:

- Your son to grasp that God is bigger and more amazing that he could ever imagine.

- Him to have a heart that wants to know God through His Word.

- Your family to become grounded in who God really is and to turn from your misconceptions about Him.

 Prayerfully watch for opportunities to chat with your son about the Truth you've both learned in the chapters you've read.

- Do you think it would be fun to go on a cattle drive? Why or why not?

- Can you think of a time when I got really mad at you? Tell me about it from your perspective.

- Do you ever worry that God is mad at you?

- What do you think it means that God the Father poured out His anger on Jesus when He was on the cross (Isaiah 53:4–6)?

- When God forgives your sin, do you think He forgets it?

CHAPTER 7:
Affirming God's Design

What Your Son Is Reading in *Lies Boys Believe*:

LIE #5: "Girls rule, boys drool!"

TRUTH: The differences between guys and girls are God's idea.

Since each of us is made uniquely, no single mold fits every boy or every girl, but up until fairly recently, everyone seemed to understand that boys and girls are different. Few parents would claim that one gender is better than the other, but anyone who has taken a quick look around a room full of both boys and girls can logically conclude that they are not the same.

But we are not parenting in logic-filled times. While our parents and grandparents certainly faced their own serious challenges, we are a generation of parents raising children in an era where many believe:

- Gender is fluid and that children should be free to determine their own gender.

- Femininity is best expressed through power. Many cultural voices espouse, for example, "the future is female."

- Masculinity is toxic and men are largely responsible for the many ills our society faces.

It's true that these are simplified versions of the sentiments many are expressing (loudly), but scan social media and you will notice these nuanced ideas presented as givens.

Because gender and sexuality have become weaponized for political and cultural gain, it can be tempting to try to stay out of the fray and hope that the deception won't seep into your son's heart. But the conversation about these issues has made its way into nearly every facet of our culture. From television shows to commercials, public libraries to billboards, wrong ideas about God's design for manhood and womanhood are seemingly everywhere. Our commitment to helping our sons ground their identity in Christ must be equally pervasive and vigilant.

In *True Woman 101: Divine Design*, Nancy DeMoss Wolgemuth and Mary Kassian provide a foundation upon which to build your son's sense of self.

> Our Creator knows us best. He's the one who knows how and why He created us male and female. As the Designer, He knows the proper way to order and fit together our lives and relationships—according to their intended design.
>
> Jesus was once confronted with a question about male-female relationships. The Pharisees wanted to discuss cultural customs and practices about divorce, and have Jesus endorse one of two popular views (Matt. 19:3–9). But Jesus took the discussion to an entirely different level.
>
> Jesus indicated that in order to get their thinking right, they needed to look beyond all their cultural customs and social conventions, as well as the distortions that had been introduced by sin. They couldn't hope to get things right by arguing over personal opinions or a list of human "dos" and "don'ts."
>
> In order to think and behave correctly, they needed to understand God's original and highest intention for man and woman. And to do this, they needed to look back to creation—to God's pattern—to understand the intent of His original design.[8]

---

8. Mary A. Kassian and Nancy Leigh DeMoss, *True Woman 101: Divine Design* (Chicago: Moody Publishers, 2012), 18–19.

If your approach to helping your son understand and embrace his masculinity is by constantly countering every wrong idea championed by the world, you're going to end up in an exhausting, and likely unfruitful, game of Truth Whac-A-Mole.

Today the message might be that masculinity is toxic. Tomorrow hyper-masculinity may be celebrated. Today, the message is that gender is fluid. Who knows when that pendulum will swing back (though we hope it's soon!) and what ideas about gender and sexuality will be espoused in the decades to come. The point is, gender matters, because God created it. And as the Creator of gender, God is the only one qualified to declare what is true.

Your son needs your help to navigate these choppy waters. The best help you can give him is the tools he needs to run to God's Word for *all* of his questions about everything, including the important questions about his identity.

Don't know where to start? May we suggest the beginning? Genesis 1:27 says,

> So God created human beings in his own image.
>> In the image of God he created them;
>> male and female he created them.

This passage is key to developing your own theology of gender and helping your boy develop his. In a single verse we find three foundational Truths:

1. God created mankind. As the designer, He gets to define our identities.

2. God created men and women distinctly different from the beginning. Boys and girls are not interchangeable.

3. God created males and females in His image. God-given masculinity and God-given femininity paint a picture of who God is to a hurting world.

Like so many other topics in this book, this will be an ongoing conversation. Our culture provides plenty of discipleship opportunities to discuss what God's Word teaches and how to respond to a world that doesn't look to Scripture for the blueprint of what their identity should look like.

Be ready! With the Holy Spirit's help and the Bible as your guide, you can help your son understand and embrace the man God made him to be. What an amazing way to live counterculturally and push back the darkness in Jesus' name!

PARENT TO PARENT

In Colossians 3:17 Paul wrote, "And whatever you do or say, do it as a representative of the Lord Jesus, giving thanks through him to God the Father."

With this passage in mind, pray for:

- Your son to want to live for God's glory.

- Your son to understand that he is a representative of Christ and that his life should look different from those who don't follow Jesus.

- Each member of your family to diligently guard his/her heart against deception in the areas of gender and sexuality and to stay rooted in God's Truth in this area.

TALK ABOUT IT TOGETHER

Prayerfully watch for opportunities to chat with your son about the Truth you've both learned in the chapters you've read.

- Why do you think God made boys and girls?

- Do you ever feel like grown-ups like girls better than boys? Tell me about that.

- What do you think it means to be an image bearer of God? How does that impact your daily life?

- What do you love about being a boy? How can we help you celebrate how God made you?

CHAPTER 8:
The Jason Davis School of Awesome

When the COVID-19 pandemic hit, like most parents we suddenly found ourselves working from home while caring for our children 24/7. It quickly became apparent that a strictly digital approach was not going to hold our sons' attention long enough to keep their education on track. So . . . we got creative.

While we recognize the importance of the traditional subjects like math, science, and reading, we also want to raise well-rounded boys who have mastered other kinds of skills like household chores, basic construction, interpersonal communication, and problem-solving.

Thus, the Jason Davis School of Awesome was born.

Capitalizing on the extra time with my boys, I (Jason) set out to teach them skills I hoped they'd use once they moved into their own homes. We built a chicken coop, learned how to forage for mushrooms, tied fishing flies, and practiced building an outdoor fire.

Though the pandemic is now in our rearview mirror and our family has settled into more "normal" rhythms of work and school, I still see my sons putting the skills they learned by working together into practice. Erin and I spend plenty of time breaking up fights and smoothing friction between our boys, but we also get to watch them cheer each other on.

Unlike our rowdy house full of boys, I grew up in a family of four with just one sibling, a sister. Though I love my sister dearly, I've always wished I'd grown up with a brother too. Watching my boys travel in a pack brings me great joy! I hope they lean heavily on each other for their entire lives.

Fostering friendship doesn't come particularly easily for me.

My perfect Friday night is more likely to involve me working on a project alone in my shop than it is going out to dinner with friends. Even so, I've had to learn that though I can *survive* without friends, *thriving* requires intentional relationships with others outside of my immediate family.

Scripture teaches that wisdom, an essential component for living free from lies, can be gleaned from spending time with other wise people. Proverbs 13:20 is a verse we've taught our sons since they were very young:

> Walk with the wise and become wise;
>   associate with fools and get in trouble.

As I read about Jesus' interactions with His disciples in the Gospels, my own hopes and dreams for my boys come to the surface. While preparing them to take the gospel to the ends of the earth, Jesus helped the disciples develop a pack mentality. He did not call them to a one-man show. Jesus Himself chose to surround Himself with other men during His time on earth. That says something to me about the value of living intentionally connected to wise Christian men and helping my sons do the same.

This is one of the reasons we've encouraged our boys to play sports. (Burning off their seemingly limitless energy is another reason!) Realistically, our sons aren't going to go on to play professional or even college sports. So, what's the point of all those hours logged, running kids back and forth to the gym? They're learning how to be a part of a team, an essential skill for the Christian life.

We often refer to our family as Team Davis. Erin will sometimes ask randomly, "Who's on the team?"

Ever eager to please, Judah will often be the first one to say, "I'm on the team."

"I'm on the team," Ezra will parrot.

"I'm on the team," Eli will say.

"I'm on the team," Noble will add.

"I'm on the team," I will say.

"I'm on the team," Erin will add as the exclamation point.

It's an exercise that takes less than sixty seconds and reminds us that God made us to depend on each other. Regardless of the size of your family, you are your son's first look at what it means to be a part of a team. Lies grow in isolation. Consistently standing in Truth requires teamwork.

One of the best ways you can help your son fight lies is by encouraging and fostering friendships with other boys, especially those who follow Jesus. Consider 2 Corinthians 6:14:

> Don't team up with those who are unbelievers. How can righteousness be a partner with wickedness? How can light live with darkness?

Encourage your son to be kind to those who don't know Jesus and to share his faith with them when the opportunity presents itself. But when he's picking "teammates," those who he will work and play beside on a daily basis, he needs more than friends, he needs battle buddies. (And you do too!)

Here's one more nugget of wisdom from the book of Proverbs. This is another verse we've encouraged our sons to memorize,

> A friend is always loyal,
>   and a brother is born to help in time of need.
> (Proverbs 17:17)

The first half of that verse is quoted often. Rightly so; learning what true friendship looks like is a lesson we all need to take to heart. But the second half of the verse isn't a throw-away sentiment . . .

> A brother is born to help in time of need.

Whether your son has biological brothers or not, whether he is shy or outgoing, whether he makes friends easily or takes a while to warm up . . . he needs other boys in his life. *He will face times of need.* If he's anything like the rest of us, he will face *many* times of need. You can prepare him for those moments and set him up for a lifetime of living in victory from lies by embracing, celebrating, and championing his need for Christian friends.

PARENT TO PARENT

Pray Proverbs 13:20 with your son in mind.

> Walk with the wise and become wise;
> associate with fools and get in trouble.

Pray for:

- God to send wise friends into your son's life

- Your son to grow in wisdom through the wisdom of others

- Him to recognize foolish friendships and turn from them

- The Holy Spirit to help your child resist pride-fueled independence and value being a part of God's team

- Yourself to recognize any blindspots in this area, and intentionally foster your own Christian friendships

 Prayerfully watch for opportunities to chat with your son about the Truth you've both learned in the chapters you've read.

- Who are your best friends? What makes them great friends?

- Have you ever heard the saying "there's no 'I' in team"? What do you think that means?

- Is there anything that keeps you from asking for help when you need it?

- Why do you think God said that it was "not good" that Adam was alone?

- What did you learn about the benefits of friendship?

- How can we help you grow closer to your Christian friends?

CHAPTER 9:
Why You Can't Wrap Your Boy in Bubble Wrap

What Your Son Is Reading in *Lies Boys Believe*:

LIE #7: "Following Jesus is boring."
TRUTH: Following Jesus is a grand adventure!

Ask my wife and she will tell you that I (Jason) am risk-averse. She's spontaneous and I'm calculated. She makes decisions quickly and easily; I tend to spend a lot of time weighing the pros and cons. She'd move our family every year or two if she could; I'm happy to stay put. It is the push and pull of our differences that make us an effective team.

Erin often describes her Christian walk as the "tightrope of terrified obedience," although, to watch her, I'm not sure she's really terrified. She seems to thrive on taking big risks in Jesus' name. I've had a front-row seat as she traveled to Alaska alone (and six months pregnant) to share the gospel with a tribe of indigenous people, taught the Bible at a conference for Hmong teenagers where she was the only one who didn't speak the language, and crossed rooms to pray with total strangers. She'd be the first to tell you that life with Jesus is never boring. I could say the same thing about life with Erin.

Even when our boys were little, my wife encouraged them to take big swings for Jesus. She's taught them to memorize Scripture, encouraged them to share the gospel with their friends, and nudged them toward every camp and mission trip opportunity that's come their way.

Though I came to Christ as a boy and surrendered my life to serve Him in vocational ministry in my teen years, mine is a quieter faith. My favorite Bible verse is Micah 6:8:

> No, O people, the LORD has told you what is good,
>   and this is what he requires of you:
> to do what is right, to love mercy,
>   and to walk humbly with your God.

For me, following Jesus is that simple. Though I have certainly felt stretched by my Savior's hand as He shapes me more and more into His image, I wouldn't describe my Christian walk as the tightrope of terrified obedience. I just try to love God and love others the best I can. It's enough.

Your son is learning that following Jesus is a grand adventure, and it is. But it's not necessarily because it always sends us to faraway lands or significant lifestyle changes. To follow Jesus is to live for something greater than ourselves. While our sin nature is always clamoring, "me first," "me first," "me first," I believe that there is something inside every man, and therefore something inside every boy, that longs to push past the limits of self-centered living and give everything we've got to something bigger.

John the Baptist (another risk-taker) described this in John 3:30: "He must become greater and greater, and I must become less and less."

John's brass-tacks summary of what it means to follow Jesus was essentially "less of me and more of Him." Easier said than done, right? This passage also gives the reason John was so willing to live beyond a life of self-seeking validation and pleasure: because Jesus is the One our souls were made to long for. He is the giver of eternal life.

I must confess that it is difficult for me to think of my role as Dad as anything other than keeping my boys safe. There is a God-given drive inside of me to protect the family that He has entrusted to me and that's a good thing. But I also know that following Jesus often comes with a heavy price tag, and that through my words and by my example, I must encourage my sons to pay it.

Consider Colossians 3:1–4:

> Since you have been raised to new life with Christ, set your sights on the realities of heaven, where Christ sits in the place of honor at God's right hand. Think about the things of heaven, not the things of earth. For you died to this life, and your real life is hidden with Christ in God. And when Christ, who is your life, is revealed to the whole world, you will share in all his glory.

Because of grace we no longer face the penalty of death for our sin. Instead, we offer a daily "death" by laying down our own rights and desires to pick up the life that God has for us.

Do I want my boys to be safe? Absolutely! What dad doesn't? But to embrace God's Truth and to help my sons do the same means to encourage them to obey Him, even when it's costly. Sometimes that means inviting the new kid at school to come to youth group. Sometimes it means missing practice to go to church, knowing it will cost them game time. Sometimes it means owning up to sin in a way that might be embarrassing. The opportunities and challenges of living for Jesus will likely increase as my boys turn into men. Through my life and my words, I seek to model that He is worth the risk.

Have you unintentionally communicated that the Christian life is about going to church on Sunday and reading a few verses before bed? Have your own fears for your child prevented you from taking risks to build the kingdom or encouraging them to? They're going to want to talk to you about the adventure of following Christ. It's an opportunity to consider how your family can ask God to pull you out of your comfort zone for His glory.

PARENT TO PARENT

Consider Galatians 2:20: "My old self has been crucified with Christ. It is no longer I who live, but Christ lives in me. So I live in this earthly body by trusting in the Son of God, who loved me and gave himself for me."

Pray for:

- God to show you what it means to be "crucified with Christ" in your own life

- The Spirit to empower you and your son to lay down your lives daily because Christ lives in you

- Help trusting God with your son's safety and future

- God to give your son supernatural enthusiasm for the Christian life

Prayerfully watch for opportunities to chat with your son about the Truth you've both learned in the chapters you've read.

- What's your idea of adventure?

- What are some of your favorite Bible stories? Why do you like them so much?

- Does being a Christian ever seem boring to you? Why do you think that is?

- Are you willing to follow Jesus wherever He leads you? Does anything about that scare you?

CHAPTER 10:
A Different Kind of Self-Control

What Your Son Is Reading in *Lies Boys Believe*:

LIE #8: "I can't control myself."
TRUTH: You have a Helper.

Would your son pass the test? The marshmallow test, that is. In the 1970s, two Stanford University researchers developed a test to measure children's ability to delay gratification. The premise was simple: a child was placed in a room with a marshmallow, a pretzel, and a bell (sounds like the beginning of a pretty good joke!). An adult explained that they'd have to leave the room for a while, but if the child waited patiently without ringing the bell or eating the food until the adult came back, they could have the treat of their choice. Variables were added, marshmallows were eaten, but at the end of the experiment and several follow-ups, researchers concluded that an ability to delay gratification as a child correlated to later-in-life successes like high SAT scores, strong self-esteem, and a greater ability to cope with stress.[9]

Though the experiment has long fascinated researchers and parents alike, in terms of wisdom, it's old news. Scripture has always championed the power of self-control in your boy's life (and in yours).

Proverbs 25:28 is a verse we've taught our own boys. Your son is learning about this verse in *Lies Boys Believe*.

A person without self-control
is like a city with broken-down walls.

In the era when these words were penned, a city without walls was a defensive disaster. Fortifications were necessary protection against the many forces that would seek to do harm. It's not much of a mental leap to consider the same destructive consequences that come into our own lives when self-control

---

9. Angel E. Navidad, "Marshmallow Test Experiment and Delayed Gratification," Simply Psychology, updated July 10, 2023, https://www.simplypsychology.org/marshmallow-test.html#SAT.

is lacking and why you probably already recognize this as an essential characteristic for your son to develop. While Scripture does use the term "self-control," it's not necessarily in the way we often mean it as a companion virtue to self-esteem or self-worth. In fact, to fully understand this "fruit of the Spirit" and best champion it in your son, it is best to strip your idea of "self" all the way down to the studs.

Value Comes from God

If this book were a conversation between parents happening in real time, we might all roll our eyes about what the so-called self-esteem movement has done for our kids. We know that the everyone-gets-a-participation-ribbon approach doesn't really equalize the playing field for everyone, nor can positive affirmations brush away the doubts and fears our child has about himself.

Your son doesn't need an identity propped up by what he thinks of himself (or what others think of him). He is a creature whose value was given to him long ago by his Creator. Genesis 1:27 teaches that all people are made in the image of God. We were made by God to show the world who God is. That's where our worth comes from and no trophy (or lack thereof) or achievement (or lack thereof) or human affirmation (or lack thereof) can strip that away.

Your son will be inclined to find his worth in all manner of things (as will you), but the search will continue until you acknowledge, and then remind yourself over and over again, that you matter because God made you. God loves you, and God has a plan for you.

Feelings Aren't Facts

Our dear friend Tippy is fond of saying "feelings aren't facts." Her point is not that feelings are bad (God created them, after all) but that they are not a trustworthy barometer for much of anything, including our sense of self. The prophet Jeremiah didn't mince words when he said,

> The human heart is the most deceitful of all things,
>   and desperately wicked.
>   Who really knows how bad it is? (Jeremiah 17:9)

Your son has feelings, probably lots of them. They ebb and flow like your own, but when it comes to lies, subjective feelings cannot be trusted to make the right call. What's more, feelings so often lead to actions, which is why the slope from lie to sin is so slippery. In teaching our sons to be their own guides away from lies and toward Truth, we miss God's warning that "follow your heart" is so often bad advice.

Self Is to Be Surrendered

Though hardly a new phenomenon, the worship of self is pervasive in our culture, yet Christ has called us to think and operate distinctly. Consider the warnings of Romans 12:2–3:

> Don't copy the behavior and customs of this world, but let God transform you into a new person by changing the way you think. Then you will learn to know God's will for you, which is good and pleasing and perfect.

> Because of the privilege and authority God has given me, I give each of you this warning: *Don't think you are better than you really are. Be honest in your evaluation of yourselves, measuring yourselves by the faith God has given us.*

So . . . if your son's feelings can't be trusted, his self isn't supposed to be elevated, and his worth doesn't depend on it, how can you direct him to, say, stop leaving the toilet seat up or not eat an entire bag of chips in one sitting or enjoy a video game for an hour and then turn it off without a meltdown? Fruit of the Spirit to the rescue!

> But the Holy Spirit produces this kind of fruit in our lives: love, joy, peace, patience, kindness, goodness, faithfulness, gentleness, and self-control. There is no law against these things! (Galatians 5:22–23)

Self-control is a gift given to followers of Jesus by the Holy Spirit. This is great news! Right now your son is learning that God doesn't want him to pull himself up by his bootstraps or try harder, but to lean into the work that the Holy Spirit is already doing in his life.

This paradigm shift requires subtle changes in the ways you communicate with your son. "Try harder" becomes "Ask the Holy Spirit for help." A battle of wills becomes an opportunity for shared humility. And while discipline has its place, when your son is out of control (or you are), it's the perfect reminder of how much you need Jesus and how essential prayer is to the work you are doing as a parent!

PARENT TO PARENT

Did you know there's a second list of fruit in the book of Galatians? (Actually, Paul wrote about it first.) It's the fruit of the flesh, a.k.a. the fruit of the "self." It's found in Galatians 5:19–21. Pray through these verses, asking the Lord to remove the fruit of self from your son's life.

Now read through the fruit of the Spirit that follows in Galatians 5:22–23. Ask God to pour fertilizer on these areas of your son's heart.

TALK ABOUT IT TOGETHER

Prayerfully watch for opportunities to chat with your son about the Truth you've both learned in the chapters you've read.

- Did you ever get so angry you felt out of control? What happened?

- Is there any other area of your life where you feel like you can't control yourself?

- Why do you think the Bible calls a man without self-control "a city with broken-down walls"?

- How can you turn to Jesus the next time you feel out of control?

CHAPTER 11:
Planting Mighty Oaks

When Noble was in first grade he came home from school with a stick wrapped in a wet paper towel. Being an all-boy household, I (Erin) didn't think much about it. I once collected nine sticks in a single pass through our house. Boys love sticks.

Noble is our most serious son. Because his mind is always in hyperdrive, his mouth rarely is.

On this day (which we later realized was Earth Day), Noble had received a small redbud sapling at school with the encouragement to plant it. When I say it was a stick, I'm being generous. No longer than a ruler, it had nary a bud or leaf on it.

On his own, without any input from us, Noble found a shovel and dug a hole right outside the window of the room where I do most of my writing. Not wanting to crush his young heart and grateful for his generosity, I thanked him for thinking of me and told him I couldn't wait to watch that redbud bloom.

That spring came and went. Summer descended with the heat and humidity so typical of our area. Then came winter. The little stick still stood tall, but I was sure it was dead.

When spring came around again, a miracle happened. My little tree, planted in faith by my little boy, sprouted the tiniest of leaves followed by miniature pink buds. It was alive! Noble hadn't planted a stick, he had planted a tree! His good intentions and loving thoughts toward his momma bore fruit. They are still bearing fruit to this day.

Your son is dwelling on a simple yet profound premise in his reading. It's wisdom passed to author Nancy DeMoss Wolgemuth by her father, Art DeMoss. As she was growing up, Nancy's dad often reminded her, **"You are who you're becoming."** In other words, the seeds you're planting now will bear fruit in your life as you grow older. God gives this same instruction to His children through His Word.

Don't be misled—you cannot mock the justice of God.
You will always harvest what you plant. (Galatians 6:7)

Part of the pressure of parenting is that you and I know this
is true. We've got eighteen years, give or take, to pour a
foundation with our child that the entire house of their lives
must sit upon. We've watched as habits, sometimes as benign
as a binky, can merge into patterns that are incredibly hard to
break. You know, but it's possible that your son doesn't.

Childhood feels eternal when you're eight, just like thirty
seems ancient. Our children have ideas about their future, but
they're fuzzy like an out-of-focus photo. It's hard to connect
the dots between the person you are in fourth grade and the
person you will be at forty, but your son is not alone. He has
you to help him; and while he may not catch a grand vision for
what his life will be like, he can learn that the seeds he waters
today will bear fruit tomorrow from your words and your
example.

Our children have been learning this lately through a lesson
I wish I hadn't taught them. More than a decade of having
children, raising children, and caring for aging parents gave
me temporary amnesia about the need to take care of myself.
Instead of planting seeds of good health, I (Erin) planted seeds
of sickness with too much junk food, too little exercise, and not
enough rest. Those seeds sprouted up as a health crisis that got
very serious, very fast.

For the past year, my sons have watched me plant new seeds. I started walking every day. Most days they walk with me. I changed my eating habits; to varying degrees they changed theirs too. I started doing cardio in our living room; they joined in. Their hearts were already young and strong (thank You, Jesus!), but mine was loaded down with rotten fruit. It's taken discipline, along with plenty of that Spirit-fueled self-control, but I've made the changes and am reaping the rewards. My point is to tell you that it's never too late to set yourself or your son on a better trajectory, back on the plumb line of truth.

Psalm 92 has been a lifeline for me in this year of learning how to become a stronger, healthier version of me. Read the promises in verses 12–15:

> But the godly will flourish like palm trees
>   and grow strong like the cedars of Lebanon.
> For they are transplanted to the LORD's own house.
>   They flourish in the courts of our God.
> Even in old age they will still produce fruit;
>   they will remain vital and green.
> They will declare, "The LORD is just!
>   He is my rock!
>   There is no evil in him!"

Don't you love this image of what our lives can look like in Christ? Flourishing. Hearty. Fruitful. What more could you want for your son?

As he considers the impact his current reality will have on his future self, help your son think through his habits, specifically the time he spends reading God's Word. That simple, daily routine of running to Truth by opening his Bible will cause a bumper crop of righteousness to grow in his life in years to come.

PARENT TO PARENT

Meditate on Galatians 6:7 again: "Don't be misled—you cannot mock the justice of God. You will always harvest what you plant."

Pray for your son to plant Truth-soaked seeds in the following areas:

- Use of time

- Study of God's Word

- Caring for other members of his family

- Rest

Prayerfully watch for opportunities to chat with your son about the Truth you've both learned in the chapters you've read.

- If we had a garden, what would you want to grow? [If you already have a garden, ask if there's anything unique he'd like to plant this year.]

- What kind of man do you want to grow up to be? How can we nurture that now?

- Are there any habits you'd like to break?

- What are some ways you can live boldly for Jesus right now?

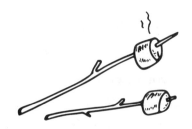

CHAPTER 12:
Now Go and Do the Same

No one is more surprised than us to see our names on the cover of this book. Though it's impossible to imagine our lives without our sons now, there was a time when we thought we didn't want kids at all. It wasn't the money that spooked us or the pull of success in our careers—we wanted to be kid-free for ministry. We saw children as a hindrance to the many ways we sought to build God's kingdom. We are walking, talking billboards for Proverbs 16:9: "We can make our plans, but the LORD determines our steps."

Through His Word and His people God has graciously shown us that *our children are a ministry.* While discipleship can take many forms, the ways we are pointing our children to Christ, and the ways they are teaching us to depend on Him, matter in ways that are much bigger than we can see right now.

You're reading this book because you get it. You acknowledge that your children are a God-given gift (Psalm 127:3) and, like all good gifts, you want to steward them well.

A remarkable reality for the Christian is that our children are also our brothers and sisters in Christ. Ultimately, they have the same calling on their young lives that we do on ours: to love God and love people and to be united in the sacred assignment of sharing the gospel with a lost world.

As your son finishes the story in *Lies Boys Believe* today, he will be challenged to embrace the Great Commission as *his* mission in life. Consider the words Christ spoke to His disciples just before His ascension and how they ripple through history into the heart of every believer.

> Jesus came and told his disciples, "I have been given all authority in heaven and on earth. Therefore, go and make disciples of all the nations, baptizing them in the name of

the Father and the Son and the Holy Spirit. Teach these new disciples to obey all the commands I have given you. And be sure of this: I am with you always, even to the end of the age." (Matthew 28:18–20)

Sometimes we make things too complicated. As He entrusted the good news to His disciples, Jesus didn't give a twelve-point sermon. He told them to do two things:

1. Go and make disciples

2. Teach the Word

We know the burdens and challenges of parenthood can be heavy. Overwhelm is constantly waiting for you right beside the pile of socks that need folding. But in the ultimate sense, you've been asked to do two things, and that's partner with Jesus to go into your home and make disciples and teach the Word. Paul's words from 1 Corinthians 3:7 come to mind:

> It's not important who does the planting, or who does the watering. What's important is that God makes the seed grow.

One parent plants. Another parent waters. Or a pastor plants, and you water. Or your parents plant and you water. Or a children's pastor plants and you water. Or you plant and they water. And then . . . you trust God with the heart of your child and He makes the seeds grow.

The New Testament records Jesus fielding questions from a lawyer about eternal life. Skilled in the art of argument, the lawyer chased Jesus' first answer with this question, "And who is my neighbor?" (Luke 10:29).

Jesus followed with the story we know as the parable of the Good Samaritan. **Read it in Luke 10:30–37.**

Jesus was teaching about caring for those who cannot care for themselves. Your son is in that position now. He's too young for a job and a mortgage. His brain hasn't developed enough for him to call the shots on his own. And he is needy, some days *so* needy.

Because of other demands on your time, there's a temptation to simply cross to the other side, to save your attention for another day. But your boy needs you today. God has given him to you as a gift. He is more than your son, and not just your brother in Christ. He is your neighbor. In loving Him well in Jesus' name you are showcasing the beauty of what Christ has done for you.

> "Now which of these three would you say was a neighbor to the man who was attacked by bandits?" Jesus asked.
>
> The man replied, "The one who showed him mercy."
>
> Then Jesus said, "Yes, now go and do the same." (vv. 36–37)

PARENT TO PARENT

Consider Isaiah 6:8:

> Then I heard the Lord asking, "Whom should I send as a messenger to this people? Who will go for us?"
>
> I said, "Here I am. Send me."

Pray for your son:

- To embrace the Great Commission in his life

- To have a willingness to love others in Jesus' name

- To be used by God to do something that lasts longer than his lifetime

TALK ABOUT IT TOGETHER

Prayerfully watch for opportunities to chat with your son about the Truth you've both learned in the chapters you've read.

- How would you describe Jesus to a friend?

- How does talking to other people about Jesus make you feel?

- Can we practice talking about Jesus?

- Do you have any friends who don't know Jesus? Can we pray for them together?

LIES PARENTS BELIEVE

LIE: "I can't/can control what my son believes."

TRUTH: **God has entrusted your son to you as a gift. While you have a responsibility to intentionally plant seeds of Truth, your son must choose to embrace God's Word for himself.**

> And you must commit yourselves wholeheartedly to these commands that I am giving you today. Repeat them again and again to your children. Talk about them when you are at home and when you are on the road, when you are going to bed and when you are getting up. Tie them to your hands and wear them on your forehead as reminders. Write them on the doorposts of your house and on your gates. (Deuteronomy 6:6–9)

LIE: "It's too soon to talk to my son about _____."

TRUTH: **The world is trying to disciple your son, regardless of his age. Now is the time to pour a foundation of Truth.**

> My child, listen when your father corrects you.
>> Don't neglect your mother's instruction.
> What you learn from them will crown you with grace
>> and be a chain of honor around your neck.
> (Proverbs 1:8–9)

LIE: "All children rebel. It's normal."

TRUTH: **By God's grace, it is possible to raise children who love Jesus and desire to obey His Word.**

> I could have no greater joy than to hear that my children are following the truth. (3 John 4)

LIE: "I've blown it as a parent! It's too late for me to teach my kids the Truth."

TRUTH: **All parents sin. That makes our families fertile ground for the gospel to take root.**

> That is why the LORD says,
>> "Turn to me now, while there is time.
> Give me your hearts.
>> Come with fasting, weeping, and mourning.
> Don't tear your clothing in your grief,
>> but tear your hearts instead."
> Return to the LORD your God,
>> for he is merciful and compassionate,
> slow to get angry and filled with unfailing love.
>> He is eager to relent and not punish. (Joel 2:12–13)

LIE: "We're too busy to read the Bible together."
TRUTH: **The Bible is God's inspired Word. It is your blueprint for how to live the Christian life.**

> For the word of God is alive and powerful. It is sharper than the sharpest two-edged sword, cutting between soul and spirit, between joint and marrow. It exposes our innermost thoughts and desires. (Hebrews 4:12)

LIE: "The goal of parenting is to raise good kids."
TRUTH: **The goal of everything is to give God glory.**

> Work willingly at whatever you do, as though you were working for the Lord rather than for people. (Colossians 3:23)

LIE: "I don't know enough about the Bible to teach it to my son."
TRUTH: **The Holy Spirit will help you understand God's Word and share it with others.**

> But when the Father sends the Advocate as my representative—that is, the Holy Spirit—he will teach you everything and will remind you of everything I have told you. (John 14:26)

LIE: "My son isn't interested in talking about God."

TRUTH: Your child (like every child) has a God-shaped hole in his heart. He has deep longings that only God can fulfill.

> He has planted eternity in the human heart.
> (Ecclesiastes 3:11)

LIE: "My son should make me happy."

TRUTH: Your son was made to give God glory.

> Bring all who claim me as their God,
>> for I have made them for my glory.
>> It was I who created them. (Isaiah 43:7)

LIE: "I wouldn't struggle with ⎯⎯⎯⎯⎯⎯, if my son would just ⎯⎯⎯⎯⎯⎯ ."

TRUTH: Parenthood is the tool God is using to expose your need for Him.

> As the Scriptures say,
>> "No one is righteous—
>>> not even one.
>> No one is truly wise;
>>> no one is seeking God.
>> All have turned away;
>>> all have become useless.
>> No one does good,
>>> not a single one." (Romans 3:10–12)

What's the story behind all those feasts?

the DEEP WELL
with Erin Davis

Dig into God's Word with
Author Erin Davis on
The Deep Well Podcast

Listen at ReviveOurHearts.com
or on your favorite podcast app.